CRISTO REY ST. MARTIN COLLEGE PREP

CHANGING SPACES

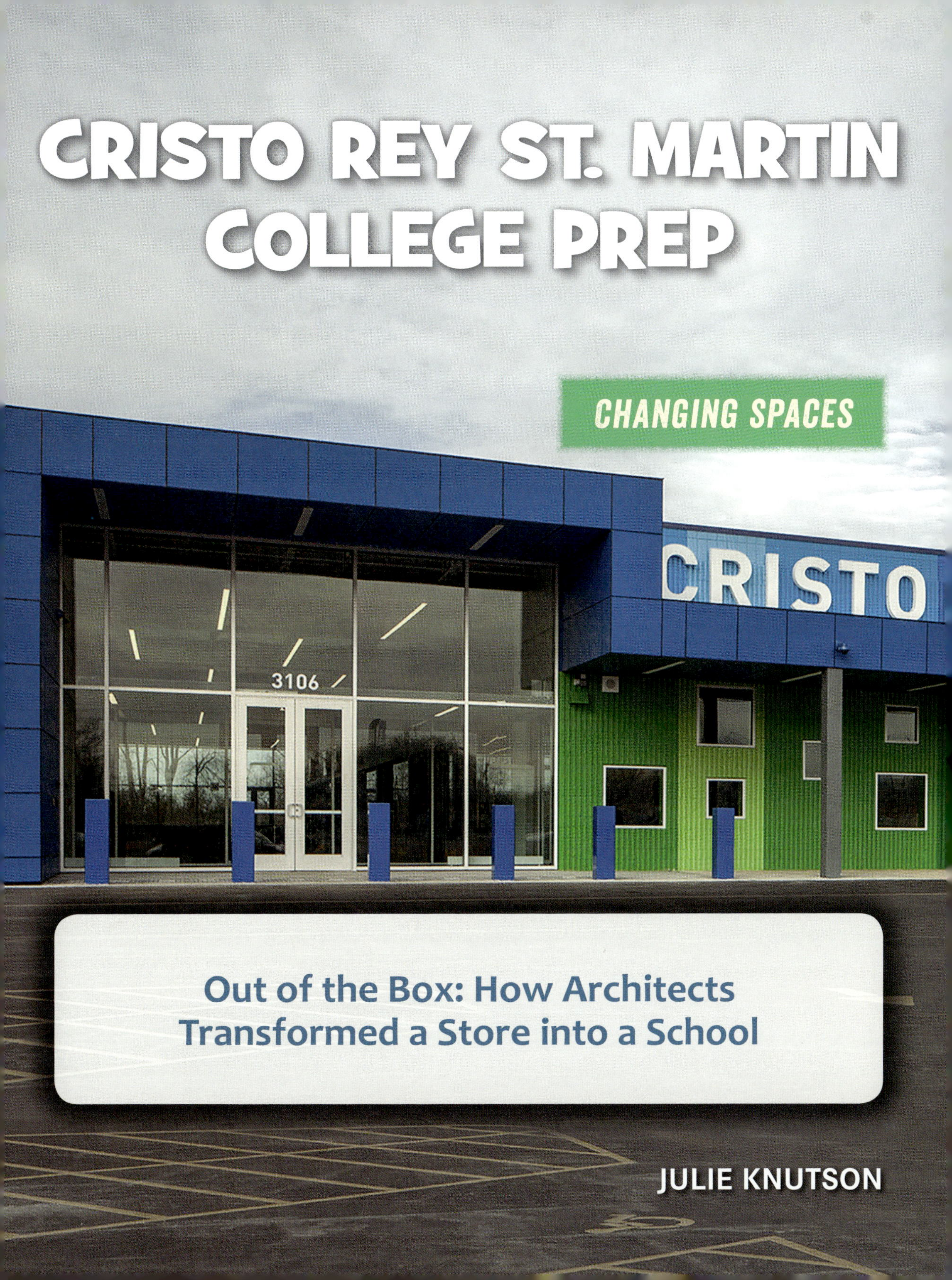

Out of the Box: How Architects Transformed a Store into a School

JULIE KNUTSON

CHERRY LAKE PRESS

Published in the United States of America by Cherry Lake Publishing Group
Ann Arbor, Michigan
www.cherrylakepublishing.com

Reading Adviser: Marla Conn, MS, Ed., Literacy specialist, Read-Ability, Inc.
Photo Credits: © Brian Fritz Photography, cover, 1, 26, 27, 28; © ezpic/Shutterstock.com, 5; © George Sheldon/Shutterstock.com, 9; © James Kirkikis/Shutterstock.com, 11; © MarieKaz/Shutterstock.com, 15; © singh_lens/Shutterstock.com, 16; © melissamn/Shutterstock.com, 17; © Sundry Photography/Shutterstock.com, 18; © Courtesy of Cristo Rey St. Martin College Prep, 21; © AProvchy/Shutterstock.com, 22; © JGMA, 23; © Adrian Coco/Shutterstock.com, 25

Cherry Lake Press is an imprint of Cherry Lake Publishing Group.
Library of Congress Cataloging-in-Publication Data
Names: Knutson, Julie, author.
Title: Cristo Rey St. Martin College Prep / Julie Knutson.
Description: Ann Arbor, Michigan : Cherry Lake Publishing, [2021]. | Series: Changing spaces | Includes index. | Audience: Grades 4-6 | Summary: "Learn more about how Illinois's Cristo Rey St. Marten's College Prep school went from vacant big-box store to bustling prep school. Explore the logistics of repurposing the space and meet the people who made it happen. The book showcases a range of 21st century skills—from "Flexibility & Adaptation" to "Creativity & Innovation"—and shows how moving away from a tear-down culture towards one of reuse helps tackle a host of critical challenges facing our planet and population. Thought-provoking questions and hands-on activities encourage the development of critical life skills and social emotional growth. Books in this series include table of contents, glossary of key words, index, author biography, sidebars, and infographics"—Provided by publisher.
Identifiers: LCCN 2020006348 (print) | LCCN 2020006349 (ebook) | ISBN 9781534169036 (hardcover) | ISBN 9781534170711 (paperback) | ISBN 9781534172555 (pdf) | ISBN 9781534174399 (ebook)
Subjects: LCSH: Cristo Rey St. Martin College Prep (Waukegan, Ill.)—Buildings—Juvenile literature. | High school buildings—Illinois—Waukegan—Juvenile literature. | Department stores—Remodeling for other use—Illinois—Waukegan—Juvenile literature. | Waukegan (Ill.)—Buildings, structures, etc.—Juvenile literature.
Classification: LCC LD7501.W3534 K59 2021 (print) | LCC LD7501.W3534 (ebook) | DDC 378.773/21—dc23
LC record available at https://lccn.loc.gov/2020006348
LC ebook record available at https://lccn.loc.gov/2020006349

Cherry Lake Publishing Group would like to acknowledge the work of the Partnership for 21st Century Learning, a Network of Battelle for Kids. Please visit http://www.battelleforkids.org/networks/p21 for more information.

Printed in the United States of America
Corporate Graphics

With thanks to Preston Kendall and Katie LaCourt

ABOUT THE AUTHOR

Julie Knutson is an author/educator fascinated by the endless ways in which people and communities can transform old spaces for new uses. She lives in Illinois with her husband, son, and extremely energetic border collie.

TABLE OF CONTENTS

INTRODUCTION
Adaptive Reuse—More Than Meets the Eye........ 4

CHAPTER 1
Low Prices and Bluelight Specials 8

CHAPTER 2
Enter Online Retailers: A Changing Economy 14

CHAPTER 3
Thinking "Out of the Box" 20

EXTEND YOUR LEARNING 30
GLOSSARY 31
INDEX 32

INTRODUCTION

Adaptive Reuse–More Than Meets the Eye

Essential Question: *Why repurpose old things, and how do we reuse things every day?*

Ever construct an indoor playground out of plush pillows and blankets? Built a bird feeder from an empty aluminum can? Crafted a perfectly strummable guitar out of paper cylinders and rubber bands? If so, you've practiced **adaptive reuse**. This unique yet everyday form of recycling involves reimagining different purposes for everyday items and modifying those items to meet that need. It requires creativity, curiosity, and a willingness to look at the objects that surround us with a mind that's open to their other possibilities.

What other adaptive reuse projects can you think of that use items found around your house?

Every day, environmentally minded and cost-conscious architects, planners, and designers seek out sites that once met a certain need to repurpose them for another. With a little imagination, teams of people help the community see what *might* be possible in that abandoned shopping mall or along that rusted rail line. While there might be a temptation to demolish these spaces and start anew, **salvaging** them carries countless benefits—from reducing waste to preserving community memory and identity. These benefits are global, rippling well beyond the borders of the immediate city or

The UN Sustainable Development Goals

In 2015, the United Nations (UN)—an **intergovernmental organization** that promotes peace and cooperation between the world's governments—launched its **Sustainable Development Goals** (SDG). The 17 SDGs provide a road map for addressing global challenges that include climate change, poverty, and access to education. A 15-year timeline was set to reach these goals. All 193 UN member-states have pledged commitment to this "blueprint for peace and prosperity for people and the planet, now and into the future."

Design solutions play a key role in reaching a number of these goals, including "Industry, Innovation, and Infrastructure" (Goal 9) and "**Sustainable** Cities and Communities" (Goal 11).

town. They provide a pathway toward creating a more sustainable world, one that more easily adjusts to change.

Sometimes, it's community members who first envision the potential in a local eyesore. This was the case in Waukegan, Illinois, where school leaders at Cristo Rey St. Martin College Prep saw promise in a vacant big-box store. The high school had outgrown the century-old structure it called home. It found abundant space in an unlikely spot: a Kmart that had stood empty for more than 4 years. Today, the school building sends a powerful message to its students. It shows that teams of people can take something viewed as having little potential and transform it into a vibrant, **innovative** space.

Construction Waste: A Growing, Global Problem

Construction waste is a major—and growing—environmental problem. According to the Environmental Protection Agency (EPA), the United States produced 548 million tons of construction-related debris in 2015. This is more than twice the amount of solid waste collected by municipal trash trucks, and that number is expected to nearly double by the year 2025.

Ninety percent of this waste comes from demolition projects. In many instances, demolished sites and the material within them could be salvaged and reused. Doing so would reduce the amount of waste in landfills. It would also save precious **natural resources**, *like wood and metals.*

CHAPTER 1

Low Prices and Bluelight Specials

By the mid-1990s, Waukegan's Kmart was one of 2,310 stores in the retailer's global empire. Residents of America's suburbs—whether in Michigan or Massachusetts, Ohio or Oregon—stood a 95 percent chance of living within a 15-mile (24-kilometers) radius of this discount superstore. During the holiday season from the 1960s on, frenzied shoppers packed parking lots and clambered for well-advertised gifts, be they Cabbage Patch dolls or Teddy Ruxpins. Whether the need was for a toaster, towel, or toy, a consumer would likely find it stocked on the shelves of this one-stop shop.

For decades, Kmarts were everywhere along suburban roadways and in shopping districts.

Kmart's origin dates to 1899. Inspired by the success of five-and-dime outlets like Woolworth, founder S.S. Kresge launched his first variety store in Memphis, Tennessee. Soon after, he opened another in Detroit, Michigan. Growth was swift, and by 1912, there were 85 S.S. Kresge stores across the country offering discounted goods. The company expanded and contracted throughout the first five decades of the 20th century. In times of prosperity, new stores opened. In periods of economic decline, such as the Great Depression, stores closed.

Boom-and-Bust Cycles

Modern **capitalist** *economies operate in cycles. Periods of prosperity—or boom periods (sometimes called bull markets)—are characterized by high consumer spending and job growth. During a downturn, or bust cycle (sometimes referred to as a bear market), people may lose jobs and investment income. This leads consumers to buy less. In early 2020, the U.S. economy suffered steep decline, falling into a bear market. The National Bureau of Economic Research reports that there have been 28 economic swings since the stock market crash of 1929.*

In 2008, the American housing market collapsed, leading to a long bust cycle.

Attention, Kmart Shoppers!

Imagine browsing the cereal aisle, debating between a box of Cheerios and Chex, when suddenly, a revolving blue light flashes. Through a loudspeaker, a booming voice announces, "Attention, Kmart shoppers. A Bluelight Special is happening in aisle 12." Customers rush past you, the clock ticking as they hurry toward this time-sensitive discount set to expire in 15 minutes.

From its introduction in 1965 until 1991, this "flash sale" was a mainstay of the Kmart experience. It was so popular that a board game called Blue Light Special—which challenged players to "Shop and Save More Money Than Your Opponents"—debuted in 1986. Of course, this item was only available at Kmart.

Though the Bluelight Special faded from stores in the early 1990s, it has been revived at regular intervals throughout the 2000s.

In 1962, the company known as S.S. Kresge changed its name to Kmart. Under this new brand, it grew at a rapid pace that ran parallel to the rise of America's suburbs. Throughout the 1970s, Kmart opened on average one new store a week. Shoppers were drawn by its low prices and exclusive partnerships with brands like Disney Kids and Martha Stewart Living. Because of Kmart's massive size, the company was able to buy in **bulk** and resell items at steep discounts. Many small, local retailers couldn't compete and were forced out of business. In 1995, the corporate giant banked $34 billion in sales, which amounts to $56 billion in today's dollars. With those profits, it began buying up other businesses, including Sports Authority and OfficeMax.

1962—Birth Year of the Superstore

Two other major retailers opened their sliding glass doors in 1962: Walmart Discount City in Rogers, Arkansas, and Target in Roseville, Minnesota.

CHAPTER 2

Enter Online Retailers: A Changing Economy

After decades of luring shoppers with unbeatable bargains, Waukegan's Kmart closed in 2013. It wasn't the chain's only shuttered store. In January 2002, the company declared **bankruptcy** and merged with another struggling brand, Sears. Between 2002 and 2017, it closed two-thirds of its retail outlets. By 2019, only 115 stores survived.

What changed in the world that led to the demise of this discount giant? Two major factors.

In the 2000s, hundreds of Kmarts across the country closed their doors.

Walmart has one of the most efficient supply chains in the world.

Target features stylish clothing brands that rival higher end items.

First, those two other retailers that also emerged in 1962—Walmart and Target—took a different approach to growth. Walmart focused on rural markets and on building a well-organized **supply chain** that allowed for rock-bottom prices and well-stocked stores. By 1990, it was already pulling in more sales per year than Kmart, despite having 600 fewer stores. Target also grew slowly but built a strong identity as a retailer that offered

Amazon bought Whole Foods for $13.7 billion in 2017. They're now able to offer shoppers Amazon Prime discounts and grocery delivery.

a department store experience without the hefty price tag. With Walmart promising the lowest prices and Target promising unique fashions, shoppers had a hard time figuring out why they should go to Kmart.

The second blow to Kmart came with the emergence of internet retailers like Amazon. As **commerce** moved online, physical stores—especially those that were aging and didn't always have fully stocked shelves—seemed like dusty relics to many. By navigating between a few screens and clicking a button, consumers could have nearly anything sent directly to their doorstep. The convenience and low prices of the virtual mall left Kmart's stores looking less appealing to savvy shoppers.

From Online Bookseller to Retail Giant

In 1994, Jeff Bezos founded Amazon.com as an online bookseller. Four years later, the company's leadership announced it would sell more than books. Today, it is the 28th-largest corporation in the world, offering everything from electronics to gourmet groceries on its virtual shelves. While consumers love the convenience, some critics have noted the company's negative impact on smaller brick-and-mortar shops.

CHAPTER 3

Thinking "Out of the Box"

After closing in 2013, the vast interior space of Waukegan's Kmart found other uses. Despite the building's leaky roof and graffitied walls, volunteer groups stored and organized donations for holiday wish lists in the former store. This was how Preston Kendall, president of Cristo Rey St. Martin College Prep, found himself in the vacant space.

Preston and his colleagues at St. Martin had been grappling with a serious problem at their school's campus: not only was their building too small, it was also crumbling at its foundations. A new space was desperately needed, but options in Waukegan were

The administrators at St. Martin were looking for a better way to serve their students.

limited. The school's administration viewed over 90 properties in search of a new campus, including old office buildings and former school sites. Nothing seemed like the right fit. Preston knew they needed to think "out of the box" to find a solution. He was on the lookout for *any* site that could possibly function as a school.

Preston saw potential in the huge empty space of the Kmart location.

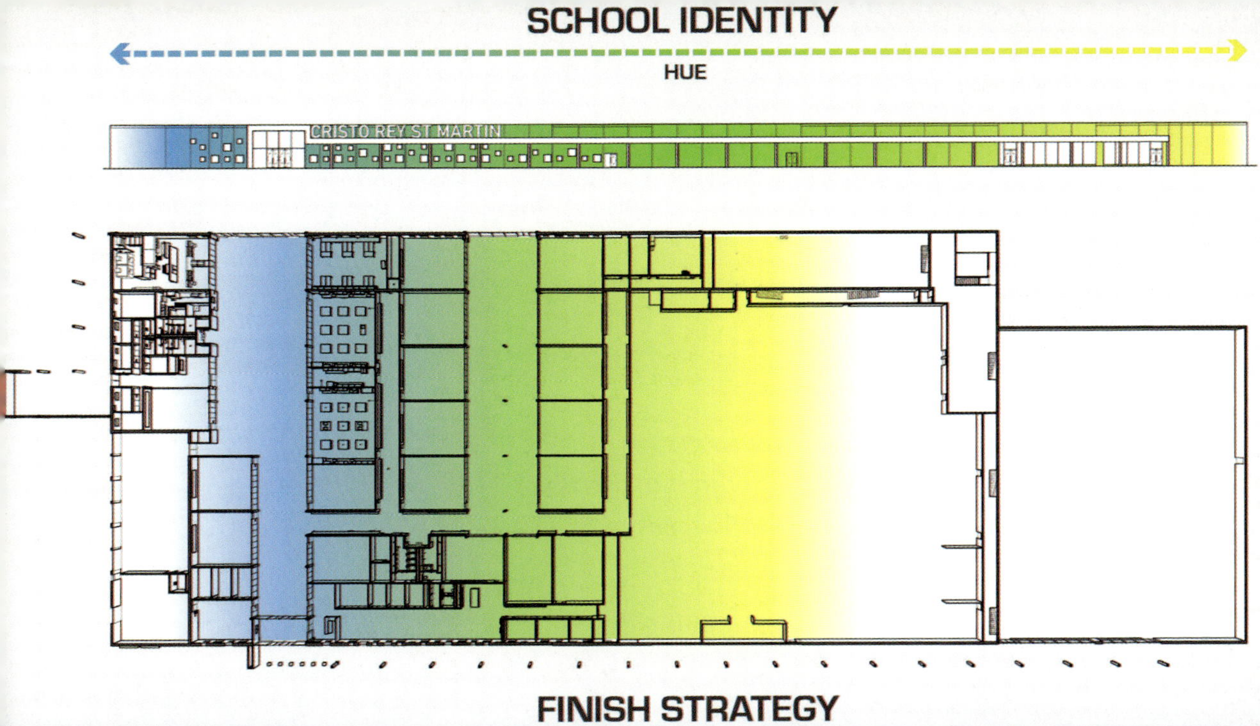

Detailed plans were made to determine whether the space could be reimagined.

And that's how, on one December day, he came to a realization. While sorting gifts alongside the school's students in the old Kmart, he thought *this* could be a school. Space to grow was the key need for St. Martin. In Preston's eyes, the abandoned store promised abundant room for expansion. He remembers, "I looked around and thought, 'There's so much room!' We could put up a few walls and turn this into a school."

Who Turned Out the Lights?

Cristo Rey's architecture firm's use of solar techniques allows for extended periods in which artificial light isn't needed. The cafeteria once went 3 weeks with the lights out without staff or students taking notice!

Preston and the school's administration approached the Chicago-based firm of architect Juan Gabriel Moreno. Their team of architects, led by Katie LaCourt, saw promise in the four walls and empty space. Katie remembers, "A lot of people would probably look at the site and not see the opportunity that we did. We saw it as a blank canvas." And even after **remediating** for mold and other environmental issues due to leaks and disrepair, they could adapt the space for just under $200 a square foot, making it more affordable than new construction.

Constructing a building from scratch can be a long and expensive process.

Designers and architects transformed the vacant space. This is the new cafeteria.

Before the designers drew a single line, they did something important: they interviewed faculty, staff, and students, asking questions about what features mattered most in a school. Katie and her colleagues knew that for the project to be successful, it would have to meet the needs of those who would use it. They used surveys and community dialogue to determine what was essential.

With that data in hand, the design team set to work on phase one of the project. Based on feedback and budget, they prioritized construction of classrooms, science labs, a library, a cafeteria, and

A library was a priority for the new school.

Adaptively reusing formally abandoned spaces can help revitalize a community.

offices. The main goal was to build a modern, light-filled center for learning. They also wanted to erase traces of the structure's former life as a discount store.

While the open canvas of a space presented opportunities, it also posed challenges. Big-box stores typically don't have windows, and at 200 feet (61 meters) deep and 500 feet (152 m) wide, the building needed to be adapted to allow for natural light. Mindful of cost and efficient environmental practices, the architects designed big slices across the rooftop to bring in daylight from above. This strategy allowed light to permeate not only the immediate spaces below, but also those adjacent. These **passive design** techniques used glass and building position to harness solar energy. The addition of massive windows to the north side of the structure further allowed for a view of a wetland located behind the site, a refuge from the busy commercial zone at the school's entrance.

The challenge of rebranding the former Kmart as a school was another obstacle that the design team embraced. Exterior features, like the store's signature entryway, were painted in eye-catching colors that announced the school as a gateway to Waukegan. Preston Kendall notes that this has been a boost to the community. People entering the city are no longer greeted by an overgrown parking lot and empty building with faded paint. Now, they encounter a "vibrant and life-giving" center of learning.

Extend Your Learning

The Cristo Rey campus in Waukegan, Illinois, isn't the only former big-box store to be adapted for new purposes. Aging and abandoned retail structures elsewhere have found new life as libraries, indoor raceways, churches, and museums. Choose one of the sites below and conduct online research to learn how other architects and designers reimagined empty stores in their own communities:

- Austin Community College, Austin, Texas (old JCPenney)
- Calvary Chapel, Pinellas Park, Florida (old Walmart)
- Head Start Early Childhood Academy, Hastings, Nebraska (old Kmart)
- Lebanon-Laclede County Library, Lebanon, Missouri (old Kmart)
- RPM Indoor Raceway, Round Rock, Texas (old Walmart)
- SPAM® Museum, Austin, Minnesota (old Kmart)

Glossary

adaptive reuse (uh-DAP-tiv ree-YOOS) reusing materials for a purpose that's different than what they were originally designed to do

bankruptcy (BANGK-ruhpt-see) the legal process for people or companies unable to pay debts

bulk (BUHLK) purchased in large quantities

capitalist (KAP-ih-tuh-list) an economic system in which trade and industry are controlled by private, for-profit businesses rather than by the government

commerce (KAH-murs) buying and selling on a large scale

innovative (IN-uh-vay-tiv) introducing new ideas or inventions

intergovernmental organization (in-tur-guhv-urn-MEN-tuhl or-guh-nih-ZAY-shuhn) a group with representatives from many countries who work together to collectively solve global problems, such as the United Nations

natural resources (NACH-ur-uhl REE-sors-iz) materials taken from the environment and used for economic gain, such as wood, water, or metals

passive design (PAS-iv dih-ZINE) using sunlight and local climate conditions to reduce the need for mechanical systems for heating, cooling, and lighting

remediating (rih-MEE-dee-ate-ing) fixing or remedying a problem

salvaging (SAL-vij-ing) rescuing or saving

supply chain (suh-PLYE CHAYN) the process of producing and distributing commercial goods

sustainable (suh-STAY-nuh-BUHL) ability to be continued in a way that doesn't use up natural resources

Sustainable Development Goals (suhs-STAY-nuh-buhl dih-VEL-uhp-muhnt GOHLZ) 17 goals set by the United Nations, to be achieved by 2030, in order to secure a future that doesn't use up natural resources

INDEX

adaptive reuse
  Cristo Rey St. Martin College Prep, 4–7
  Kmart, Waukegan, 23–29
  retail structures, 30
Amazon, 18, 19
architects. *See* Juan Gabriel Moreno

bear markets, 10
Bezos, Jeff, 19
big-box stores, 7
Bluelight Specials, 12
boom periods, 10
budgets, 26
bull markets, 10
bust cycle, 10, 11

capitalism, 10
commerce, online, 19
construction waste, 7
Cristo Rey St. Martin College Prep
    adaptive reuse, 4–7
    designing, 26–29
    search for new site, 20–23

daylight, 28–29
demolition projects, 7
design techniques, passive, 29
designers, 26

economics, 10
environmental practices, efficient, 28
exterior features, 29

feedback, 26
flash sales, 12

glass, 29

internet retailers, 14–19
interviews, 26

Juan Gabriel Moreno, 24
design goals, 26–28

Kendall, Preston, 20–24, 29
Kmart
  history of, 8–13
  store closings, 14–19
Kmart, Waukegan, 7, 14
  adaptive reuse as school, 23–29
  rebranding, 29
  uses after closing, 20–21
Kresge, S.S., 10

LaCourt, Katie, 24, 26
landfills, 7
light, artificial, 24
light, natural, 28–29

natural resources, 7

recycling, 4
remediation, 24
repurposing, 4, 5
retail structures, 30
  See also big-box stores
reuse design challenges, 28

salvaging, 5, 7
Sears, 14
solar, passive, 24, 29
solid waste, 7
superstores, 8, 13
supply chains, 16, 17
surveys, 26
sustainability, 6, 7

Target, 13, 17, 19

United Nations Sustainable Development Goals (SDG), 6

Walmart, 13, 16, 17, 19
waste, construction, 7
waste reduction, 5
Waukegan, IL, 7
Whole Foods, 18
windows, 28, 29